Project Management:

Failed IT Project Business Cases,

A Career Guide to Lessons Learned

Natalie Disque, PMP

DEDICATION

I would like to first dedicate this book to my husband who always puts up with my workaholic work ethic, listens to me wonder where the logic is to many IT projects I work on, and who always inspires me to go after my dreams. Thank you from the bottom of my heart.

Second, I would like to dedicate this book to Brandon Olson at The College of St. Scholastica (www.css.edu) for allowing me to pursue my teaching passion as an adjunct faculty member since 2005. Creating and teaching courses for CSS has allowed me to pass along my real-world experience and knowledge to my students. It has been truly an honor to work for you and I hope to continue to do so for many years.

Third, I would like to dedicate this book to all my past, current and future students. May the business cases I discuss in this book help you to better understand what can go wrong in an IT project and how to avoid these types of failures when you are a PM for an IT project.

And lastly, I would like to dedicate this book to all PMs out there. Please review my lessons learned and feel free to email me with additional thoughts you may have. After all, we are all learning from each other and can improve upon the IT project successes by sharing our lessons learned with one another.

CONTENTS

Subscribe to my list to get discounts on my upcoming
Project Management books!

http://forms.aweber.com/form/60/605157960.htm

Natalie Disque, PMP

Subscribe to my list to get discounts on my upcoming
Project Management books!

http://forms.aweber.com/form/60/605157960.htm

Natalie Disque, PMP

ACKNOWLEDGMENTS

I would like to state that I do not have anything personally against nor have any connection to any of the companies and projects listed in this book. They were included for the sole purpose of more current IT projects that I can present to Project Managers to learn from.

1 The Purpose of this Book

After many years of being a Project Manager (PM) for both small to large companies, along with creating and teaching online Project Management classes since 2005, I have read about far too many IT projects that have failed due to reasons that could have been prevented. As I go from semester to semester teaching about Project Management and reading my students assignments about failed projects, it amazes me that the PMs on the projects haven't learned from past failures. Don't get me wrong, there are times where an IT project fails due to business decisions or programmer errors. Ultimately, though, the responsibility lies with the PM running the project.

After doing research of my own and reading about how many failed IT projects there have been in just the past 10 years, it lead me to the following questions:

- Did the project fail due to a communication breakdown or was it a glitch in the software or an outage on the servers?

- Could the project failure been prevented? If so, by the stakeholders or the PM?
- Are IT projects failing due to PM's not improving their skills by learning how to proactively take charge of a project, communicate effectively and lead a project to succeed?
- Does the PMI offer enough webinars and courses on the topic of leading successful projects versus learning from failed projects?
- Are PM's not taking enough initiative to research past failures and understand how they can avoid the mishaps from past failed projects?

When assigned to a new project, I would think that a good PM would do some research on similar projects either in the company's past documentation or online to see where successful actions were taken, as well as what constituted in the project failing and what actions could have been avoided.

When I started doing my own research on the subject of failed IT projects, I realized that there is no shortage of information available online. However, instead of having a plethora of failed projects listed all over the Internet to have my students go research, I decided to put together in one place a small collection of business cases about different IT projects that have failed in the more recent years. Even just focusing on the past 10 years alone produced far too many failed projects than I expected. This small research endeavor of mine took on its own legs and lead to this book being written.

Since I have spent most of my years in the IT industry, the focus of this book will be on failed IT projects. I do know from teaching students working in other industries that there are many healthcare, construction, and government PMs

that have engaged in failed projects as well. Therefore, my goal is to create business case books for those industries following this book. Stay tuned!

Overall, it is my hope that current and future PMs will read these case studies and lessons learned to take preventative measures in their own projects and help businesses from failing in the future. I believe that learning your trade never ends, regardless of the industry. Reading about more case studies where projects have failed and understanding what went wrong and what could have been done to correct the problem will create a better success rate not only for PM's in the industry, but also for the organization they work for. Let's learn together and raise the success rates of IT projects.

Natalie Disque, PMP

2 Introduction

Technology is an integral part of our lives. Whether we want to stay connected 24/7 or not, we are hooked on it with little hope of ever weaning away from it anytime soon. This is particularly true with the current younger generation growing up with technology as a normal thing in their everyday lives.

I do not know many teenagers who are not constantly using their smartphones to update their status on some type of social media platform, let alone do I know of any that watch television or listen to the radio to get their latest news as my generation did growing up. This generation is connected more than we probably want them to be, but it may be a good thing in regards to the experience they will have to continue innovative thinking and moving technological advances forward in the future.

Technology has always changed rapidly throughout my early career life in the 1990's through early 2000's. But it seems to change at the speed of light these days, or at least that's how it appears. The laptops are getting thinner and more powerful, some of which now have removable keyboards, turning them into super-powered tablets. The smartphones have larger screens, better sound and picture quality, and faster Internet connections. There is literally a new smartphone with better features being introduced to the market through all mobile carriers every 6 months, making your current smartphone antiquated by the time you have figured out how to use all its features and are ready for an upgrade. Due to these fast-paced changes, the marketability and usability of electronics is of the utmost importance.

For the sake of market demand, as for the sustainability of an IT project, the design of a project is amongst its most important factors. This probably serves as the reason we live in a world where we tend to focus on the IT projects that are successful – the projects that make the news and a subsequent social movement, changing the game by their sheer existence. The IT industry is constantly pushing harder and faster to keep up with the "instant gratification" world we live in, which leads to more and more IT projects forming, as well as more and more IT projects being rushed and failing.

In the shadows of all these successes, however, are a lot more IT project failures. In fact, for every IT project that is successful, there are probably a dozen more projects that either never saw the light of day or did not have what it took to survive and flourish in the brutal technology world. It may or may not come as a shock to you to know that hundreds of IT projects fail each year. Yes, there are *that* many projects being developed and tested. The successful IT projects you hear about in the media are the true minority. Only the strong survive, and the brilliant rise to the top.

One would think that with the billions of people in the world, and the constantly changing regions of the world, all of which are at different paces and starting from different points, that it would make the technology story a totally different one than what you hear. It would be easy to see how someone would think that no matter what kind of IT project is released onto the market, that surely, somewhere, anywhere on this earth, and through the avenues and dark alleys of the online world, there would be a market for it that could be cornered and monopolized. However, it is not quite that simple.

Stated simply, the IT world is cutthroat. You have to be selling a product that people want now and a product that is more impressive than what the next company is offering. Developing an IT project that goes on to be successful is more work than simply designing a system and then releasing it. It is not as simple as getting all of your friends to post it on Facebook or Instagram, or getting a hashtag trend going on Twitter. Although this will help get your brand in front of many people, it probably will not get you the kind of momentum you are looking for with your project.

Much of the success of an IT project is dependent on one person and one person only: the Project Manager. Because of the consistent supply and demand for Project Managers, the IT industry is far from suffering from a shortage of employees. However, finding qualified Project Managers, like PMP certified ones with years of experience, is a better solution.

President, Sharavon Goli, of IT job finder website Dice.com, says that, "Growth in project management as a category that remains stable, with a depth and breadth of demand across almost all vertical markets and with positions available in 46 or 50 states across the U.S. Salaries remain well above average -- $106,000 per year compared to an average IT salary of $85,000 for all other tech professionals." [1] One thing is for sure, if a Project Manager has a vision, and the skills and know-how to pull off an IT project success, they are probably going to be worth their weight in gold in today's technology-dependent world.

Goli is also quoted as giving advice about what can make a Project Manager's IT resume stand out. The fact of the matter is that a plain resume just will not get you noticed nowadays. Competition is just too fierce and too many people can do what you do or even better. When it comes to this industry, Goli says, "What has changed is the qualitative side. As Project Managers' roles shift, they are expected to take on additional responsibilities above and beyond the fundamental scope of managing each IT project. The role has evolved over time, and there are a few trends that may be infringing on the Project Manager's core job description." [2]

Being a Project Manager myself for many years, I tend to agree. Looking at what a Project Manager's roles were 5 years ago has evolved over time. Although one thing has remained the same – it is the Project Manager's main job to keep the project on track and not lose site of the end goal. This is often hard with different delays in timelines, budget cuts and scope creep that play a factor throughout the life of the project. Nevertheless, the Project Manager needs to keep the project on track, even around the changing triple constraints. The positive outcome of IT project failures is that it makes for better Lessons Learned. With each project failure, Project Managers and businesses learn how to avoid similar outcomes moving forward.

CEO Kevin Kern of project portfolio management firm Innotas has plenty to say on the role of Project Managers. From Kern's point of view, it seems like successful Project Managers have to wear several hats: "Project Managers aren't just project-based, they're supervisors. They are managing solutions and applicants, as well as managing the software developers, and there aren't enough developers, ever. So, Project Managers are being asked to take on so many responsibilities that their job description gets blurred."[3]

There are probably a million and one roles somebody could put on a list that are the responsibility of a Project Manager to ensure any project is a success. On top of this list, however, the main responsibility, in a nutshell, of a Project Manager is to deliver and do so in a way that benefits the sponsor and lives up to their expectations. Here is a short(er) list of the roles of a Project Manager:

- Progress
- Cost
- Quality
- Performance (Value)
- Cash Flow
- Safety, Health & Environmental standards

- Regulatory
- Reporting
- Risk
- Change [4]

The list is not all inclusive in any manner, but it is a good starter for writing a career guide for those interested in a career in project management. In addition, there are probably a dozen or so mini-lists that this list could be broken down into because the role of the Project Manager is just that important.

In order to really get a good look at how important a Project Manager's role is, you have to look at some of the bigger failures in IT project. Yes, the failures. We live in a world where we often put more attention and focus on learning from the successes. Sometimes, though, the successes are simply the people or concepts that can make the most noise.

Learning from failures can be even more rewarding in life, and doing such with IT projects is no exception whatsoever. After some of the biggest failures as of yet in the IT industry are discussed, we will delve into the reason that these kinds of projects fail.

Shall we begin?

3 J.P. Morgan Chase & Co.

Using tools as a driving force to complete work is something all IT projects are accustomed to. Microsoft Excel, one of the more popular applications used, can be a great timesaver for many projects due to its ability to add formulas and make your calculations easier.

Within Excel, there is a feature to use calculations across an entire spreadsheet where one would simply plug in the formula (i.e. =SUM(a1+b1+c1) which would add up all values in cells A1, B1 and C1 and display the product) and then copy the formula across an entire row or column and magically watch all numbers within that row or column update according to the calculation entered within the cells.

Excel's formula feature, although very helpful in large spreadsheets, can also present a huge problem. As with any application or system, an incorrect entry (what I like to call a "user error") can botch a lot of information because the calculations are repeated throughout an entire row or column, therefore, the spreadsheet displays incorrect calculations when one number is entered incorrectly. This can be a huge risk to an organization that doesn't catch this snafu in a timely manner. This exact blunder is what happened to one of the largest financial institutions, J.P. Morgan Chase & Co., which unfortunately for them, caught worldwide attention. This incident was called the "London whale" incident and happened in 2012.

Excel was the tool of choice used to create what was called a "Synthetic Credit Value at Risk (VaR) Model" to help the J.P. Morgan Chief Investment Office understand the level of risk they were exposed to when managing the bank's financial hedging strategies in the derivatives market.

The project was a simple copy and paste of multiple spreadsheet which should have helped automate financial figures to provide a trader advice on bets to make in the market. This trader was called the London Whale, the nickname for the J.P. Morgan's London Chief Investment Office whose actions were said to have had such a large impact that it moved the market. However, the Excel spreadsheet he was using at the time to provide market advice had incorrect calculations copied over throughout the spreadsheets. Due to no due diligence being incorporated in verifying the calculations, the project produced a loss in trades totally upwards of $6 billion, which to date is probably the largest monetary loss for a project using Excel.

There were apparently six issues identified as the

contributing factors to this failed project. Quoting from the
report, the investigating committee found:

1. "Inadequate resources were dedicated to the
   development of the model. The individual who was
   responsible for the model's development had not
   previously developed or implemented a VaR model,
   and was also not provided sufficient support – which
   he had requested – in developing the model.

2. The model review policy and process for reviewing the
   new VaR model inappropriately presumed the
   existence of a robust operational and risk
   infrastructure similar to that generally found in the
   Firm's client-facing businesses. It thus did not require
   the Model Review Group or any other Firm unit to
   test and monitor the approved model's
   implementation. Back-testing was left to the
   discretion of the Model Review Group before approval
   and was not required by Firm policy. In this case, the
   Model Review Group required only limited back-
   testing of the new model, and it insufficiently
   analyzed the results that were submitted.

3. The Model Review Group's review of the new model
   was not as rigorous as it should have been and
   focused primarily on methodology and CIO-submitted
   test results. The Model Review Group did not
   compare the results under the existing Basel I model
   to the results being generated under the new model.
   Rather, it theorized that any comparison of the
   numbers being produced under the two models was
   unnecessary because the new model was more
   sophisticated and hence was expected to produce a
   more accurate VaR.

4. The model was approved despite observed operational problems. The Model Review Group noted that the VaR computation was being done on spreadsheets using a manual process and it was therefore "error prone" and "not easily scalable." Although the Model Review Group included an action plan requiring CIO to upgrade its infrastructure to enable the VaR calculation to be automated contemporaneously with the model's approval, the Model Review Group had no basis for concluding that the contemplated automation would be possible on such a timetable. Moreover, neither the Model Review Group nor CIO Risk followed up to determine whether the automation had in fact taken place.

5. The CIO Risk Management played too passive a role in the model's development, approval, implementation and monitoring. CIO Risk Management personnel viewed themselves more as consumers of the model than as responsible in part for its development and operation.

6. The CIO's implementation of the model was flawed. CIO relied on the model creator, who reported to the front office, to operate the model. Data were uploaded manually without sufficient quality control. Spreadsheet-based calculations were conducted with insufficient controls and frequent formula and code changes were made. Inadequate information technology resources were devoted to the process. Contrary to the action plan contained in the model approval, the process was never automated." [1]

Lessons learned: Excel is an excellent tool that needs careful monitoring that tables and formulas are copied and pasted correctly from worksheet to worksheet within a spreadsheet file. It should not be the PMs responsibility to do the actual verification of the cells, unless the PM is the one who created the template and distributed it out for use. All employees should be shown some of Excel's awesome features, such as pivot tables, calculations, and sorting, with the caveat of knowing they need to check their work!

4 McDonalds ®

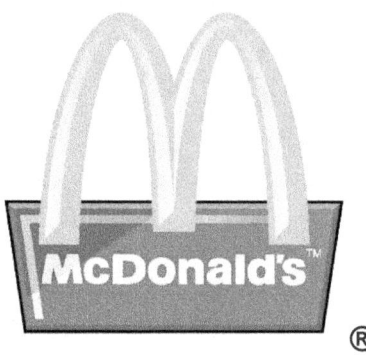

®

The golden arches is more than just hamburgers and fries. It consists of one of the largest food franchises, which obviously needs a leading architecture to handle all the millions of orders coming in each day and to be the forerunner for the industry. Think about it – they need to track items like sales, service time, staff, supply data, vendor locations, equipment and its repairs. This takes a complex IT system.

Back in 2003, after the company disclosed its first unprofitable quarter ever, McDonalds® planned to spend $1 billion over a span of 5 years to tie all of its operations into a real-time digital network. This large project would have been the most expensive and extensive IT project in the history of the company.[2] The purpose of the project was to provide the company's management with detailed information such as:

- how many billions of burger patties, buns and chicken nuggets were being consumed at any or all stores at any time of the day in order to ensure that customer service was being provided in the time frames the company had set out (i.e. a 3 minute service goal)
- if the oil fryer in any given restaurant was turning out French fry stick at the proper temperature and time
- if the carbon dioxide in the soda tower in a given restaurant had fizzled out

Why would they need this detailed information? To return to its roots of being the fastest and most consistent fast-food service in the industry.

The project failed before it even took off due to the fact that McDonalds® is in the fast food industry, not the technology industry and they needed to focus on being more creative in their products and services. Looking at the menu, the Big Mac, their signature sandwich, was over 35 years old and did little to keep up with the changing times of the consumer's evolving tastes. Relying on the Big Mac to bring in profits grossly inflated the arrogance of the company.

The solution was to create more relevant menu items, such as healthy options for those who don't want fried foods. I don't normally eat at McDonalds® but can tell you that I have seen the healthier options available on its current menu, such as fruit as a side for children. I can also tell you that although they still do have the "super-size" type of meals, the chicken wraps are a good healthy alternative and actually taste pretty good as well.

The project of maintaining a billion dollar network was deemed impractical from a financial standpoint. The final result was that their expertise of developing and mass-producing burgers and fries had little relevance to the IT world of integrating and implementing a real-time network. Albeit that the technology efforts of McDonalds® has not all slide by the wayside. They have, over the years, focused their innovations on improving the customer experience by speeding up the counter and drive-through trips, accepting credit and debit card payments, and using the Internet to post training information for their employees. [2]

Lessons learned: Although McDonalds® needs to do little to remain in existence for years to come, they need to make sure, like most businesses, to focus on their roots – being the best fast food restaurant there is. This may mean changing up the menu items to keep up with the health industry. This may mean better customer service at the drive thru. This may also mean a faster process of making burgers or fries. No matter what the verdict, the end result is they are not a technology company nor do they need to be on the cutting edge of technology. People just want their food and fast, whether fried or healthy. Just give them what they want, plain and simple.

5 Nike ®

®

I hated to write about Nike® when putting together this book on failures because I am a big Nike® fan and only buy Nike® sneakers due to their quality over other brands, at least in my opinion. As anyone who has a son that is into their "shoe game" knows, Nike® is known for their expensive and high-demand "Jordans" (and I don't mean the most current Jordan's either – the older ones like 2003 – 2010 are big sellers in my neck of the woods).

Nike®, known best for its apparel and footwear, especially by famous athletes like Michael Jordan, have had failed IT projects just like anyone else. Nike's ® supply chain project in 2001, which was supposed to drive the manufacturing of its sneakers down from nine to six months, was a good idea to stay ahead of the competition. However, a glitch in their demand planning software with factory orders (where it ignored some orders and duplicated others) created a big problem.

Something as small as a computer glitch and not doing enough testing of the system affected the performance of such a large company because it was too slow, had bugs, and employees were not trained properly before the system went live.

"Nike® spent $400 million dollars updating their supply chain system and ERP implementation. They were surprised to find that what it got them was a ghastly 20 percent dip in their stock, $100 million dollars in lost revenues and a myriad of class action lawsuits. Where did they go wrong? They implemented a new demand-planning software solution without testing it, and everything went awry. Rather than helping Nike® match their supply with demand, narrowing their sneaker manufacturing cycle, they ended up ordering low-selling sneakers in place of high demand ones, collapsing the supply chain." [3]

The reason I decided to include this project in my book is for a few reasons.

1. It shows how important testing a system prior to implementing it into the production environment is.
2. It shows that no matter what company you are, all employees who will use a new system need to be properly trained on how to use it.
3. Using an old model may need to be analyzed to verify it complies with today's market.

The project did rebound due to a great business plan for an

overall supply chain project that was understood at every level of the company. (Ahem...Business majors take note – you WILL use your business plan teachings in the real world after you graduate!).

There were workarounds built, data was downloaded and manually reloaded into the supply chain system, quality assurance personnel and business people tested the system frequently, and consultants were brought in to build databases to bypass portions of the application.

The lesson learned for Nike®? Nike's ® move to its SAP ERP system provided a better solution, even though it needed to be heavily customized to fit into Nike's® legacy systems.

6 Apple ®

®

Believe it or not, Apple® has had IT projects fail. Although they have risen above the creation of just computers, their innovative thinking has led to frenzies with their technological demand of i-products. Although the phone service providers do not usually allow us to trade in our old phones for the latest smartphones each time a new one comes to market, there is always those that need the latest and greatest from the technological giant, causing prices to skyrocket and stocking of the devices to be on backorder.

As if this instant gratification world that we live in isn't fast enough, when Apple® unveils a new product, they provide a live stream of the event on their website. As some of us will never understand why some folks will post every event of their lives on social media, neither will those same folks not understand how we could not possibly be tuned in to every update that Apple® has to make. However, when you have a high demand product, such as the latest smartphone, you are bound to encounter failure rearing its ugly head around the corner. This is precisely what happened in late 2014.

Apple's® live stream of the unveiling of the iPhone 6 and Watch presented users with difficulty in watching the actual unveiling due to code on Apple's® website page. Without getting too technical, Apple® made some changes to their code for the live stream so that the website page would be more interactive with the users. In doing so, live tweets about the event were supposed to display on the page. However, this additional Javascript code led to a disaster because of issues with the page's cache.

The apple site with the new code was refreshing itself so often (every few milliseconds) that it removed the ability to have the information cached, which is what helps your computer keep the current information settings. With the page being un-cachable, there was a huge negative impact on the performance of the page in regards to loading the contents and the live streaming.

Apple's® website also has videos that are embedded into the page's code. When the performance problems with the live stream crashed, it also affected the videos. In fact, if you tried to load the page during the live stream, the browser would have just stopped working. This is certainly not the result Apple® was anticipating for a launch of its new products!

Apparently, this was not the only issue that day. Due to all the refreshes of the page called by the Javascript, it downgraded the quality of the video. As if that also wasn't enough, apparently there was a foreign language translation part of the code to help with different viewers in different countries tuning into the unveiling. The encoder for the foreign language and the live streaming were not in sync, so many viewers saw the video overlaid by a foreign language track. In some instances, viewers just got the good old message of "Could not load movie" or "You don't have permission to access". I'm sure frustration set in on both Apple's® end and the viewers end. [4]

Lessons learned on this project? I believe there are many. First, as in any IT project, the new coding should have been tested out in lower environments or at the very least, on a parallel production server that is only accessible internally. This way, they can test it first and verify the new code works prior to releasing it live to the entire world.

Second, they should have confirmed the amount of storage they would be using to refresh the page every few milliseconds could be handled on their storage servers. Was there a risk plan in place for high peaks? I don't know but think there probably wasn't. They should have made sure to set up their storage correctly, or at least had a mirror of the servers to cut over to as a backup, to handle the amount of streaming so the website didn't crash.

Third, when you are introducing multiple changes to code, make sure that not only they each work independently, but that they also work interdependently.

7 Sapphire iPhone Screens

Here is another Apple® failure for something that I believe any smartphone owner is looking for – an unbreakable screen!

Let's face it, one of the biggest complaints that iPhone users have is that the screen cracks and looks like a spiderweb from hell if dropped just once without a Lifeproof or Otterbox surrounding the phone.

Apple® had a great project idea with screens made of a super-hard and transparent substance that would make it more indestructible than the world is used to. This substance? Sapphire crystals.

This $1 billion project to introduce what everyone is looking for – harder screens – failed from the start when it built a sapphire factory before the technology for the iPhone was even complete. Talk about putting the horse before the cart!

According to MIT Technology Review, Apple® literally hired "GT Advanced Technologies, a developer of innovative ovens, to cook sapphire crystals. But the company had no experience producing crystals in commercial quantities, or meeting Apple's® famously demanding timelines." [5]

The result? To produce the sapphire crystals, it takes about nine months, which is too long to wait in order to include them in the newest iphones. In addition, GT Advanced Technologies failed to produce any meaningful quantity of sapphire that was usable. In order for sapphires to be produced, a very clean environment is required but ongoing construction at the factory meant that sapphire was grown "in a highly contaminated environment that adversely affected the quality of sapphire material." [6] Talk about a disappointment and big project failure! However, apparently the sapphire crystals were used in making the Apple® Watch, but online sources state they did not use GT Advanced Technology as their supplier. Smart move, Apple®.

Lessons learned: Apple® needs to find a substance to build its iphone screens from to eliminate the cracking. I believe that everyone who owns a smartphone would even pay more to get that feature! If it can't be done from sapphire crystals, then they need to find an alternative substance and plan for a trustworthy supplier to provide them with what they need prior to wasting money on another project that doesn't guarantee the quality and quantity they need for their always in demand products.

8 Google Glasses

I am not sure if you remember this project, but Google, the leader in online search engines created Google Glasses, which were exactly what is sounds like – glasses you wear that allows you to browse the Internet. These computerized glasses allowed you to use the Google engine to view maps, emails and even take pictures and videos!

Thinking about this concept, I can think of a bunch of ideas that this type of invention would be good for. Having accessibility to Google maps right next to your eyes may help with bright glares of a GPS from your car dashboard at night. It would provide you with the ability to look up directions while you were driving, enabling you to keep your eyes on the road and following directions next to your head at the same time. (Of course, I am assuming you can multi-task while you are driving. This assumption comes from watching people eat while they are driving anyway, leaving only one hand on the wheel and their eyes only half on the road and half on the chicken parmesan sandwich that is about to drip in their lap).

On a funnier side, I am envisioning reading emails while someone boring is talking to you, all the while, they think you are listening. (This could come in handy in a work meeting, as I am sure you are reading your phone under the table anyway).

On a more serious note, I am also envisioning taking pictures or videos while at your child's sporting or school event without having to carry an additional camera. You could capture a snapshot of a car accident you are in and then possibly send it to your insurance company since the Google browser is already part of the glasses. You could even video a conversation with someone to reference later. (This would come in handy for those who can't recall names easily).

The Google Glasses project sounds like it would be a very innovative one (especially with my previous ideas listed). However, with a cost of $1,500 USD per pair, I am not sure how many common folks would be rushing out to buy one. It also doesn't help when the Google company co-founder, Sergey Brin, began not wearing the glasses in public anymore. [7]

The project itself, labeled "the computer you wear on your face", may continue in the future (you never know, the people at Google may read this book and take my ideas into consideration). But for now, the project has come to a

screeching halt, with developers completely stopping work
on the apps for the product and launch dates postponed.

Lessons learned: First, get input from consumers on
features. I am sure there are a ton of great features a
wearable computer can have and people want, but do we
necessarily want them all impairing our vision? Second,
collect market data on the amount of money a consumer will
spend on such a device. If after looking at the expensive
iPhones that run upwards of $800 for the most advanced
products seems okay with the public, then try to stick to that
dollar amount as the high end of the spectrum. If the
features you offer on the product cannot be lowered to that
amount, then make a base model product with additional
features as "add-ons" for an additional cost. If someone
wants to browse on glasses but doesn't want email popping
up in their vision, then don't include it in the base version. If
someone wants a camera for stills and video, add it as an
upgrade, but at a reasonable price. Do surveys and find out
what that price point is. Don't just release a cool new
technological toy that 80% of people cannot afford.

Lastly, what happens to those who have prescriptions?
Would the Google glasses go over our existing glasses? This
sounds like a bulky alternative to just having a normal GPS
or smartphone with us to do all the same things.

9 Bitcoin

If you haven't heard of Bitcoin, don't worry about it. It is basically an electronic currency created for all countries, with no central bank and looked to be promising when the project began. They call it the "crypto-economy". For most of the world who has shopped online, we are used to merchants like Paypal or authorize.net to accept our online payments. Bitcoin was supposed to be the next big thing.

According to the MIT Technology Review, *"The idea of Bitcoin remains intriguing—a peer-to-peer currency with no central controller, instantly transmitted anywhere, and powered by a clever cryptographic engine. But in practice, it is more like a Ponzi scheme that attracts speculators, and it's become the payment form of choice among professional cybercriminals.*" [8]

When the project first started and the Bitcoin was initially launched, it was presented with a huge problem – drugs! Criminals were using this online currency in exchange for illegal drugs and the founder of Bitcoin was arrested! We have already looked at IT projects that fail, but to have your project be overcome with criminal activity is not a good thing you want your name attached to.

Lessons learned: Just like the other innovative products that companies come up with, you need to survey the consumers to see what are the most important features to provide in your product that consumers are looking for? Maybe there is a futuristic world where we don't carry money in our wallets and everything is paid for online with a cryptocurrency. Who am I to say? The project seems like a new innovative way to pay for things online, but I personally am not sure I trust a different currency than the one I currently use – good old fashion US dollar. You can read more about Bitcoin on their main website: https://bitcoin.org

10 Sainsbury's

British Supermarket giant Sainsbury also joins the list as having a major fail in the IT world. The corporation's goal was to install an automated fulfillment system with the company's Waltham Point Essex distribution center, as Waltham Point served as the distribution center for a lot of London and Southeast England. Increased efficiency with a barcode-based fulfillment and streamlined operations were Sainsbury's goals. However, one of the biggest features of the product would cause its biggest failure. [7]

The system was installed in 2003 only to quickly run into

issues and errors reading barcodes. Call me crazy, but isn't reading barcodes in a supermarket the whole purpose of a system? Don't fret, however, because Sainsbury claimed in 2005 that the system was running just fine – as intended. Within two years, however, Sainsbury scrapped the entire warehouse project. The total cost wrote off for Sainsbury due to the project's failure? 150 million pounds. For a little perspective, that comes up to about $265,335,000 if you use today's rate of exchange.

Lessons learned: Once again I have to go to the reason of testing prior to deployment. If the system was properly tested in a lower environment, any kinks would have been worked out. In addition, if you let problems go unaddressed when the product rolls out, those problems become big problems and will only get worse overtime.

11 Foxmeyer

FoxMeyer Drugs was among the top brands in pharmaceuticals in the United States in 1993. In fact, the company's net worth was a whopping $5 billion. However, like any other growing company, FoxMeyer wanted to increase efficiency. Therefore, the company bought an SAP system, a warehouse automation system, then hired a consulting firm to get everything going smoothly. All in all, everything was supposed to cost $35 million.[9]

FoxMeyer Drugs was bankrupt by 1996. A competitor swooped in and purchased it for $80 million. When taking a closer look at FoxMeyer's failure, you can see that they put an unrealistic and aggressive timeline into place as the entire system was supposed to be up and running and in use – everything switched over and going well – within 18 months. The second mistake FoxMeyer made was the use of such a system threatened the livelihood of the people who worked there. Therefore, they were not supportive and onboard with the automated system. The company would go on to see three existing warehouses closed down, the initial warehouse to undergo automation was plagued with rashes upon rashes of sabotage. Inventory was damaged by workers; orders went unfilled.[10]

All in all, the system wound up being far less capable than
the one it was created to replace. The SAP system was only
processing 10,000 orders on a nightly basis – 10,000
compared with 420,000 orders it had been processing. To
explain the reason for the project failure, FoxMeyer has also
been quoted as saying that one reason was because
Anderson, the consulting firm, and SAP used the ERP
program as a training tool rather than putting their best
workers on the project.[11]

Within a few years, the news would be even sadder for the
entire FoxMeyer Corporation. The company filed for
bankruptcy and was in full-blown lawsuits with Anderson
and SAP. In fact, FoxMeyer was suing them each for
$500,000. The company claimed that the cost had come to
twice the estimate. By 2004, all lawsuits were either settled
or just dismissed.

Lessons learned: Make sure that your timeline is not too
aggressive to the point of being unrealistic. In addition, don't
put all your business into one basket; meaning, ensure your
company has a plan to survive if one of its projects fails.

12 Australian Airlines

An outage of any system can be catastrophic, let alone one that monitors airplanes. In September 2010, Virgin Blue had to do things the old fashion way – manually. The airline used an outsourcer called Navitaire for their reservations and check in system. When the system had an outage, it left thousands of passengers stranded and 116 flights cancelled in one weekend. [13]

The issue was resolved in the morning, and even with the airline providing hotel accommodations to hundreds of passengers who were stranded outside of their home town, I am sure there were a lot of angry passengers! Think about how long the lines in the airport must have been when the operators behind the counters were entering in the information manually. Certainly the airline workers must have wanted to quit or hit the bar for a stiff drink shortly after this failure occurred!

I am not sure when one can find a good time for a hardware test in the airline industry, but there at least should be backup servers or a system running parallel to the live system in another location. This is just simple Risk Management 101 – a contingency plan!

Lessons Learned: Have a mirror of your systems running at all times in a separate location than your current live system. I stress a different location because if a natural catastrophe is what causes the outage, you don't want all your systems located in the same place. You will want them in different physical locations (preferable across many states).

And for goodness sake, never take the servers down when it hasn't been communicated to the users! They will not be ready for an interruption in their work day and the screaming will never end!

13 Lessons Learned

You have just read about how common it is for an IT project to fail. In fact, there are studies that even say that the average failure rate for these kinds of projects is somewhere between 50 percent and 80 percent. Seems feasible, doesn't it? All you have to do is think of the possibility of twenty projects you didn't hear about and match them with one that you did.

Organizations, however, have picked up on this possibility of failure and are starting to be more proactive about it when it comes to their IT projects. This interest has gone so far that there are a lot of companies that require a lessons learned session for each and every project – a move that has definitely led to a better and bigger understanding of why IT projects fail.

Failure of an IT project will often have more than one real cause. Failure is often a mixture of many causes that all came crashing down too soon. The fact is that a lot of IT projects are full of problems. So, in light of all of that, let's take a long look at the most common reasons that an IT project fails, from different standpoints...[12]

14 Requirements

Requirements

System and user requirements are essential for the success of an IT project. As much information as possible needs to be communicated so everybody involved will know what the system needs to be efficient. (I always stress this in my classes because communication is KEY to success in any project!) Not only does communication of the requirements benefit the user, but the creator will also be better able to cater a product toward what its potential users are actually capable of doing with it.

The following are some of the reasons IT projects fail when it comes to requirements:

1. **Unclear Requirements**: Inadequate and unclear requirements can trigger IT projects to fail big time. The last thing a Project Manager wants to do is to allow a project to go through with

requirements that are so vague that there is too much room for interpretation. Although it is usually the Business Analysts job to create the requirements and break them down to be clear and concise, in cases where the requirements are vague, Project Managers or developers wind up having to fill in the blanks. IT is a business and you want to leave as few blanks as possible to be filled in at any time. Unclear requirements should be unacceptable prior to a project starting.

2. **The Gap**: A project doesn't want to leave a gap between the IT system's requirements and what is expected of it. Here is where expectations are exaggerated and the project will find that its users start to imagine and hope that the system is going to do things that simply are not captured as part of its requirements, ultimately giving the users a sense of the project failing.

3. **Non-compliance**: The requirements of IT projects have to be compliant with the law. Just like any other industry, there are laws, standards, and regulations that have to be followed. On top of these are best practices and requisite audits. As part of the planning process, it is best to make sure all the laws are laid out on the table so the company will really know what it is getting into, and what legal troubles down the road it would like to avoid at all costs.

4. **Failing to Consider Integration**: Requirements need to truly analyze the project from an enterprise level. This simply means that Project Managers need to take into consideration how the IT project will work with important

business processes. In addition, integration needs to be considered with how well the program will work with processes that are vital to the business functioning as a whole.

5. **Not Bringing in Experts**: Experts are needed when coming up with an IT program's requirements. Time needs to be taken with designing a system's projects. The best thing to do is to bring in Subject Matter Experts, or SMEs, for simple, but not so simple, consultation.

6. **Looking for a Problem**: In some cases, some technology is just a solution that is simply looking for a problem. For an IT project to truly be successful, the requirements definitely need to solve a problem that businesses and companies have in the first place. In order to really figure out what the requirements of the system would really need to be, the stakeholders of an IT project need to know what problems need to be solved so they can cater their product to those issues.

7. **Drifting**: When the requirements simply do not go with the business case, an IT project can be headed right down the drain. Requirements need to stay on track with the project's original goal. The point is: stay focused on whatever you're offering, and take that into consideration with how you continue on and better your product.

8. **Architecture is controlled by Requirements**: When requirements cause a solution, this is not good for an IT project. The correct architecture must be in place for the IT project to work. There is no sense in getting the right resources and plan in place if the architecture is not available. The requirements will tell what

architecture will be needed in order for the project to be successful.

9. **Misguided Priorities**: One thing that is classified as high priority with requirements is when they are considered nice-to-have. A company's priorities need to be accurate for the success of an IT project. [13]

15 Business Case

The following are some of the reasons IT projects fail from the Business Case standpoint:

1. **Not analyzing alternatives**: The entire business case does not consider different ways of looking at the project, which can cause failure. Later on down the road, projects can face challenges and can leave the Project Managers and other team members asking themselves why they didn't consider a certain approach. It is possible if that approach had been different, the fate of the project may have also been different.

2. **Lackluster Financial Vision**: Plain and simple, if the business case has faulty financial expectations, the bucket is going to leak

somewhere. The difference is the company that is smart and really monitors its financials, as well as the price of the project, will be able to track if the business model will be able to continue after a failed project. Realistically, you'd like to be a billionaire in a year. However, how likely is it really to happen?

3. **Optimism Bias**: In a lot of ways, optimism bias ties into lackluster financial vision that we just discussed. The main difference is it focuses more on the way people like to think overly positive. Thinking positive is great, but you have to have a plan if something negative happens. You need to stay grounded; stay thinking realistically. Business is not accurate, but the better you can really gage the reality of your expectations, the better you just might do. You'll be better prepared and can handle countering whatever happens.

4. **Fake Numbers**: When coming up with a financial analysis, you should be as objective as possible. Business developers can make up numbers; they can pull all sorts of tricks to make numbers "work" and look good on paper. Looking good on paper doesn't count for anything once a project is in the drain because of "cooked" numbers in its financial forecast.

5. **Metric Based Approvals**: Yes men do the company no good when it comes to a project failing. Furthermore, a company is only doing an injustice to itself when it had a bunch of reviewers who approved a business case with only partial forecast metrics. Risks need to be examined, and don't forget about constraints. Just because the

road looks smooth does not mean that some of the obstacles ahead cannot be foreseen.

6. **Overlooking Future Costs**: Everything sounds great when a business case tells you that it is going to decrease existing costs. However, everything will not look so great when new costs pop up from the project – costs that nobody seemed to anticipate. A great example of this is a system that increases a company's need for system administrators while doing the good deed of decreasing the use of administrative resources.

7. **Not a Business Case in Sight**: Last but not least, when it comes to where an IT project can fail due to the business case, the failure can actually be the lack thereof one. Somehow, someway, the project went on without any formal analysis or examination of its purpose and ability to stand. [14]

16 Planning Reasons

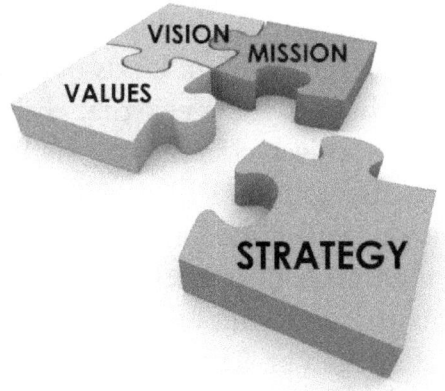

As expected, failure for an IT project can be looming in how the project is managed. Every other factor could have been right, and examined beforehand. However, if a project is just not planned right, everything else can tumble down with it.

Let's look at the Project Planning reasons that an IT project would or could fail:

1. **Budget Mishaps**: Even if you're just rolling in the money, it is still good to make moves on a budget. If you don't, the next thing you know may be that you don't have a budget because you've

"exhausted your resources" – code for run out of money. Financial chaos is one thing you can plan on with an IT project when the budget has errors.

2. **Lackluster Risk Analysis**: Risk is a part of life, and it is certainly a part of business. Any move you make involves some risk. While a lot of risks may indeed not be foreseeable, there are probably just as many that can be seen if you analyze the situation. With an IT project as well, it is best to go one step beyond analyzing the risks and make sure that the risks are communicated with all those involved on the project.

3. **Not Identifying Stakeholders**: An IT project has to undergo different kinds of clearances and whatnot, like anything else that costs money. One way an IT project can fail is by the Project Manager not getting IT operations involved. This can run a project into a major roadblock because once the time comes for the project to launch, the person in charge of operations could reject the project altogether. The only way to really describe this kind of fail is: the ultimate backfire.

4. **Rosy Resource Assumptions**: For an IT project to be successful, it has got to have as much attention as humanly possible. Simply put, you cannot plan to commit 100 percent of your time to a project when you are well aware that you have other projects or commitments. This is sure to come out in the progress of the project – progress which will definitely be behind estimations because said estimates were based on putting in 100 percent work.

5. **Optimistic Estimates**: When estimating what a project will need to get off the ground, run, and

keep on running, your estimates have to really be based on reality. You have to plan for the unexpected, as well as be prepared for the missteps that will happen along the way. The true scope of the project has to be taken into consideration for estimates to even occur and be accurate.

6. **Sabotaged Estimates**: Another way of thinking of these kinds of estimates is as being estimates that are coerced. These are estimates where the Project Manager tells the team to come up with lower estimates, which may in turn make the project seem more appealing to stakeholders. An example of this would be asking someone to estimate the cost of something, then telling them that you cannot imagine it costing more than such-and-such. This kind of language is going to imply what price range you're looking for and that they should come up with something that will be appeasing to you. This is not good when reality sets in.

7. **Naivety**: People providing estimates for an IT project need to be intelligent and at least have some good level of experience in the field. Knowledge is power and you will need all you can get to get an IT project to be successful. Last thing you want is a Project Manager's naivety rearing its ugly head down the road in the form of a failed project.

8. **Ballpark Figures**: Rough estimates make due just fine if you're sending a ten-dollar bill to the store with your child and what you're getting will cost between one and two dollars. However, with

IT projects, ballpark figures just won't cut it in the end. The danger with rough estimates is how they are assumed to be concrete, meaning that any move made from then on is solely based on the presumed-to-be-true estimate. (Think the assumption of the numbers being "written in stone").

9. **No Critical Thinking**: It is not uncommon for tasks that are not on the "direct" path to success to be overlooked. However, failure to really estimate those tasks that don't seem as important can lead to big trouble down the road for an IT project. An example of a commonly overlooked task would be data migration.

10. **Poor Scheduling**: You have to decide who is going to do what tasks and when is everybody going to do it. Technology is possibly the fastest moving factor in our day-to-day lives. That makes it all the more important to have everybody and everything in their place, with whatever other off-springs needed in place as well.

11. **A Big Release**: A great way to reduce risk and cost is by releasing an IT project in phases. However, what is even more interesting, is the number of IT projects that are planned to come out with big bangs.

12. **Lack of Tactic**: A project can and will fail if it is carried out following an ad-hoc process word-for-word. During the process of project managing, it would behoove the Project Manager to look at its methodology and see if the entire concept, and all of its components, even makes sense. [15]

17 Execution Factors

Executing a project is only one component of having a successful IT project. However, project execution is very important – maybe just as important as everything else. Once everything else has been planned, and signed off by the appropriate stakeholders, twice as much attention needs to be paid to the project's execution.

Let's look at several common project execution mistakes:

1. **Outdated Plans**: Project plains have to be kept up to date. (I'm talking updated daily!) This is probably even more important during the execute phase of an IT project. The negative result of this could be the project becoming obsolete, therefore leading the project to go on without a plan. Any project believed to be successful without a plan might as well plan to fail. It rarely works.

2. **Not Tracking**: Tasks needs to be tracked. Project Managers cannot wait until deadlines were yesterday, or last week, to pay attention to the schedule issues. This is how a project will quickly become behind schedule. And behind schedule leads to be over budget.

3. **Neglect**: Issues must be managed. Neglect of a project occurs when Project Managers fail to stop certain issues from getting bigger. It is the role of the Project Manager to resolve issues before they escalate and become real problems that threaten the success of the project as a whole.

4. **Failing the Scope**: As mentioned before, for an IT project to be successful, the real scope of the project has to be accurately estimated and the progress has to be managed. The plan has to be stuck to; changes have to be handled and handled in a positive way for the system. One quick way for a project to go into disarray is through what people call "scope creep." It is not a good thing when problems or additional requirements creep up on you and potentially extend the length of the project. Don't let scope creep happen! Set the expectation early on that once sign off is sent, no additional requirements are accepted into the release.

5. **Risk Coming to Life**: Okay, it is sometimes potentially good when a risk that was brought to light during the planning phase is coming to fruition. This does show that at least the resource that identified the potential risk is pretty good at predicting what many might consider the unpredictable. However, certain risks coming to fruition may just be big enough to sink the project into the abyss of being a failure. A great example of this happening is if a resource dependency was predicted and now that resource is becoming scarce – the resource being a human, let's say. If this "resource" gets sick or decided to quite one day, the risk has been "realized" and the project could very well fail. In addition, this ties into an earlier failure reason we mentioned, which is estimating the resource at 100% when in reality, they are working on two projects simultaneously and therefore are really only dedicated 50% of the time to each project. This estimation of the availability of the resource is a big risk.

6. **Lack of Financial Control**: One role of the Project Manager is to make sure that the project's budget is under control. Money is an issue, even when you have plenty of it. This is all the more reason for watching the wallet closely and the budget even closer.

7. **Performance Issues**: An important team members' failure to perform well does indeed affect the success of an IT project. There may be 100 small positions under the umbrella of the project. However, everyone else starts to notice the weight when that one, seemingly insufficient

person, is suddenly not in the equation, or that person is not pulling his or her weight toward the finish line. If the person's role isn't all that small, the project could very well fail.

8. **Lacking Communication**: Communication is key in any project, and is probably ten times more important in a massive and expensive IT project. Stakeholders need to see everything from progress to objectives to quality to risk and every bit of information that happens to fall in-between. When important people can't see this information, expectations start to get a little blurry when compared to reality.

9. **Displeased Customers**: Yes, the customer is indeed always right. This is even true when it comes to IT projects and their customer satisfaction. A low customer satisfaction rating can be disastrous for an IT project and any of its components. This very factor makes it important that Project Managers and those involved on the project not only design a product that will benefit the user, but also be in tune with what the user really needs and works hard toward catering the product to that information. [16]

18 Business Factors

The business of an IT project and its impact on society is also important to its success. While IT systems are a part of a greater vision, the business of the system must be well-planned and understood. However, business also includes exterior reasons and things that affect a project – any project.

Now, let's look at some of the reasons and IT project fails

when looking at the business side of things:

1. **Changing Strategy**: A project cancellation can come up for a lot of reasons. One of these reasons is a change and different direction of the business strategy. Priorities change for any business. In light of this, it is beneficial to a Project Manager to really analyze, assess, and envision what types of priorities could shift in some way that the product can be catered toward that change.

2. **Market Environment**: Everything can go right with a project. However, all of this will not matter if the business environment changes. These changes can be in the form of new laws or even a recession or depression that affects the market so greatly that an IT project becomes unwanted, not needed, or totally obsolete. A good Project Manager will take a close look at the business environment to see where and how the IT project fits in to that environment.

3. **Changes in Organization**: There can definitely be a rift in a project rolling out when there are organizational changes. The set-up and flow of an organization has a great impact on a project's success. Even smaller changes in an organization can have big impacts down the road and lead to an IT project crashing and burning.

4. **Disruption**: There is often a lot of resistance to launch, and for many reasons. Important business talent is needed with their great time and effort being required for an IT project's launch. However, if business is interrupted, the possibility of an IT project being successful can be disrupted as well. What makes this kind of interruption so

risky within the scope of the project is that
important talent could drop out of the project or
see that their specialty is better needed elsewhere.

5. **Low Reception**: If users are just not interested
   in adopting the technology or the process, the
   struggle to success will be an uphill battle for an
   IT project. The simple fact is that people have to
   be interested, and sometimes this interest has to
   be built up by the managers of the IT project so
   that people are more likely to be interested.

6. **Sacrifices**: Too many sacrifices in the quality of
   the product can affect how well it is perceived by
   the public, as well as how the product performs.
   One key thing to remember about business is that
   it favors a quick, inexpensive project. Sure,
   companies sign off on the risk that a project might
   have issues with quality. However, having too
   many negative dings about the quality is not good
   either. If the quality of the IT project suffers in too
   many places and in too many ways, the company
   can expect a product that is perceived as being
   unusable.

7. **Bad Results**: The results of a business decision
   can never truly be 100 percent predictable. The
   reality is that the Project Managers have to plan
   for business not going as well as everyone
   involved would hope. A product can be delivered
   exactly to specifications. However, the results
   might not meet expectations. An example of this
   would be a product that results in a decline in
   sales rather than an increase.

8. **Force Majeure**: A Force Majeure is simply
   something that no matter how smart you and your

team are and how much planning you all do, the failure of a project can still result because it is up against uncontrollable factors, like a war breaking out or a natural disaster. At the end of the day, neither one of those things care or will take into account the needs and wants of an IT project. [17]

19 Political Factors

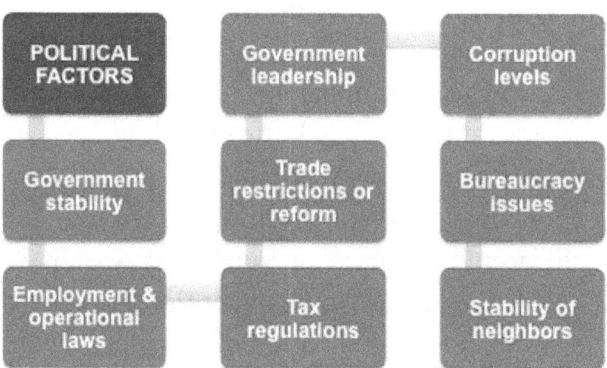

Political factors also affect the success of IT projects, in part because the company has to adhere to the law of the land and laws do change. However, the following reasons have more to do with the politics within the actual project rather than outside of it. Let's take a look:

1. **Sponsorship Change**: If a sponsor decides to change his or her mind about the IT project, you can expect there to be some issues that arise because of it. In addition, if the sponsor is a big ($$$) sponsor, their pulling out could even

influence the entire project to fail. If at all possible, a Project Manager should try to establish a good relationship with as many sponsors as possible, while at the same time doing things to focus on the needs of the current sponsors to try to keep them onboard.

2. **Missing Executive Support**: There are indeed powers that are bigger and badder than the sponsors. The typical thing to watch out for when a project is failing is when these larger powers can step in to pull the plug on an IT project. This almost always spells FAIL for any IT project.

3. **Undercover Moves**: It is not uncommon for an IT project to fail because of sabotage. This sabotage can indeed come from within, such as from a stakeholder. Unfortunately, we live in a world where many people, if not most, are out for their own personal gain. A stakeholder can be no different and in doing such, this person can purposely do things that hinder the success of a project for their own benefit...whatever that particular benefit may be, as it will not always be clear to everyone else.

4. **Vendor Relationship Mess-up**: A project's relationship with a vendor is important to the success of the product because vendors are the people who get the product out in front of the potential consumer. Issues with a project can quickly start to add up when the project's relationship with vendors go sour, all the more reason to be nice to the guy who is selling your product, especially if you cannot sell it yourself.

5. **Vendor-to-Vendor**: People often overlook this issue, but there are times where vendors

themselves can be having issues amongst each other. Issues for an IT project can start to pop up here and there when the relationships of various vendors are on the frets. While there may not be a lot a company or Project Manager can do about this, he or she can at least look at these sorts of relationships and the directions in where they may go and what kind of impact they will have on the IT project.

6. **Interpersonal Conflict**: Conflict between people on the team, no matter how big or small their roles are to the greater picture, can ripple away from the meeting tables and affect the success of a project. First and foremost it is important to understand that everyone involved in a project must be on the same page. Ego's need to be checked at the door. [18]

20 Technical Factors

Last, but not least, let's take a look at the technical reasons that IT projects tend to fail. As this type of project is mostly based on how well it runs and what it can do, the actual technical attributes can cause the project to sink or swim in the long run:

1. **Uninformed Technology Choices**: IT projects can fail when a business chooses certain kinds of technologies without really understanding what the implications of their respective design are. As a part of planning, and marketing, Project Managers should have a full grasp of what the design of a

certain kind of technology is intended to do and how that role factors into the bigger picture.

2. **Bad Evaluation**: Thorough evaluations must be done before any kind of technologies are chosen to be used as part of the IT project. Here, bad decisions can lead to the failure of an IT project because technologies that don't fit the goal of the system are used, leading to further issues down the road.

3. **Lackluster Design**: Technology is a lot like a building. For a building to be attractive, it has to be architecturally appealing as well. The project issues that can pop up when this occurs really cannot be counted, so it is best to just try to avoid them altogether by having a design that is technologically appealing for the current market.

4. **IT Governance**: Project Governance helps make sure that a project is executed according to the standards of the company. Governance keeps all project activities above board and ethical. It creates accountability. Not having an IT project use project governance could cause a project to fail.

5. **Losing Technical Resources**: Above all, if the project is going to be successful, a Project Manager should have a backup for an important technical resource. Cross training works well to help this situation. The last thing in the world the project needs is for a resource on which it depends to suddenly be unavailable.

6. **Technical Dependencies**: This is the phase of the project where things can really get delayed. Technical dependencies tend to be big roadblocks

in an IT project. The Project Manager needs to document the technical dependencies to try to forecast where the roadblocks may occur and possible workarounds.

7. **Gold Plating**: Gold plating is when developers add in features that simply are not compatible with the requirements and are more "extra features". Gold plating can lead to an IT project failing. This additional complexity grows and starts to affect a project's costs. Even worse, it can cause a user to simply reject the product altogether because it is too difficult to use, or the components simply do not make sense or were not asked for in the first place.

8. **Vulnerability**: IT projects are just like a store, meaning that they too can fall prey to hackers and other kinds of security issues. The information system of an IT project needs to take this into account during its design since certain kinds of security vulnerabilities can surely lead to risk and delays that the Project Manager nor stakeholders would have imagined for the project.

9. **Planning Failure**: The capacity of a project needs to be planned for so success is more likely. When capacity is not taken into account, a product can fail significant amounts of performance tests. Furthermore, it can continue to require information technology that is simply outside of the project's budget.

10. **Tool Fallouts**: Tools are an important component of an IT project, and their breakdown can lead to a major project failure.

11. **Faulty Testing**: The goal of testing a product before it goes into the live environment and

reaches the consumer is to see what kinds of
issues, like defects, could arise once the product is
actually in use. Inadequate testing is a major issue
that cause IT projects to fail. These problems not
only create frustration amongst the potential
users, but they can also cause the project to have
delays. As we have already leaned, delays in the
project lead it to potentially going over budget. In
addition, inadequate testing also plays a major role
in a user's confidence in the product/system.

12. **Lack of Methodology**: Even in the processes of
an IT program, the overall concepts and reasoning
behind everything will need to make sense for the
project to continue and see any sort of success.
One of the biggest technical reasons that IT
projects fail is because there is no methodology to
what the Project Manager is doing and why he or
she is making the choices they are making. [19]

21 Conclusion

Regardless of which actual business system and planning criteria of an IT project is not planned for or is overlooked, the components of a project all play into one another to help the project become a success. Aside from the numerous listed reasons for IT projects failing, there are still many other ways that they can fail, as well as a few big things that Project Managers can do to help the failure be either less impactful or be something that simply doesn't happen at all.

A steering committee that is carefully selected is one thing that every IT project needs to have in place to be successful. This committee should be led by a senior business executive who does not serve also as the chief information officer. It is also worth mentioning that this steering committee should also include senior staff members whose occupations are from areas or lines of business that would be affected by the particular system being created. If not, then business changes should be delivered in such a way that meets expected benefits.

For IT projects, especially large projects, to be successful, there must be a strong hand controlling everything that involves the stakeholders. This hand should pull into the equation outside expertise that is totally unbiased and unrelated to the organization and its subsequent politics. If a project is very large or what many would consider to be high-risk, it can be perfectly acceptable to include staff from other departments of the organization (a.k.a. "lines of business"). It would even behoove the project to include technology experts who are outside of the organization (a.k.a. consultants). The advantage of bringing in consultants is that they can bring to the table outside perspectives that can help the success of a project because when you are too close to a project, you can't have an unbiased opinion. In addition, these types of people can also help keep the decisions made by the steering committee in check with reality, even going as far as challenging or questioning the committee's decision.

Another important factor in the success of an IT project is taking broad project reviews seriously. Big IT projects should definitely be under the microscope of regular project review. Regular reviews are the objectives of many project management approaches. However, these reviews are also focused on time in many instances, as well as cost and how closely the project meets with original requirements.

These kinds of reviews should keep their focus on assessing whether or not the original benefits of the IT system are even still accessible and achievable. In addition, they should try to answer whether or not the benefits have changed in some way or if they are even of enough importance to the organization and its goals. Factors like a changing market or economic conditions should be considered. Changes in technology should also be considered, as well as the current social climate, as these are all factors that can affect the success of a project.

For these kinds of reviews to be effective, Project Managers, and others involved in the processes of the IT project, should work toward having a steering committee that is diverse. Diversity is vital to the success of the project and making sure that the reviews are wider and more inclusive of many different kinds of concepts. A lot of research into failed IT projects shows that in too many instances, there is too much reliance on processes instead of more work being put into establishing good, strong leadership and the inclusive engagement of individuals who are actually interested in the project and its goals.

Above all, Project Managers and companies looking to invest a lot of valuable time into IT projects and systems can really benefit from simply learning from the past. Just like governments and many social elements of the world, a lot of social progress can be achieved when the powers that be look at the past and actively try to learn from it. For major IT projects to be successful, the projects have got to have an overall control that is strong. Its approach needs to involve every stakeholder, while also drawing in the expertise from outside people who are unaffected by issues within the company.

22 Footnotes

1. http://calleam.com/WTPF/?p=5517
2. http://www.baselinemag.com/c/a/Projects-Supply-Chain/McDonalds-McBusted
3. http://blog.360cloudsolutions.com/Top-Six-ERP-Implementation-Failures
4. http://blog.streamingmedia.com/2014/09/why-apples-livestream-failed.html
5. http://www.technologyreview.com/news/532636/why-apple-failed-to-make-sapphire-iphones/
6. http://www.technologyreview.com/news/532636/why-apple-failed-to-make-sapphire-iphones/
7. http://www.technologyreview.com/featuredstory/532691/google-glass-is-dead-long-live-smart-glasses/
8. http://www.technologyreview.com/review/524691/marginally-useful/
9. http://www.computerworld.com/article/2533563/it-project-management/it-s-biggest-project-failures----and-what-we-can-learn-from-them.html?page=4

10. http://www.computerworld.com/article/2533563/it-project-management/it-s-biggest-project-failures----and-what-we-can-learn-from-them.html?page=4
11. http://www.computerworld.com/article/2533563/it-project-management/it-s-biggest-project-failures----and-what-we-can-learn-from-them.html?page=4
12. http://www.information-age.com/it-management/outsourcing-and-supplier-management/1286558/australian-airline-grounded-by-it-failure
13. http://www.computerworld.com/article/2533563/it-project-management/it-s-biggest-project-failures----and-what-we-can-learn-from-them.html?page=4
14. http://management.simplicable.com/management/new/64-reasons-that-IT-projects-fail
15. http://management.simplicable.com/management/new/64-reasons-that-IT-projects-fail
16. http://management.simplicable.com/management/new/64-reasons-that-IT-projects-fail
17. http://management.simplicable.com/management/new/64-reasons-that-IT-projects-fail
18. http://management.simplicable.com/management/new/64-reasons-that-IT-projects-fail
19. http://management.simplicable.com/management/new/64-reasons-that-IT-projects-fail

ABOUT THE AUTHOR

Natalie Disque is a PMP certified, full time IT Project Manager who has worked in the IT department for many clients such as Capital One, Bank of America, Wells Fargo, Prudential Relocation, and Johnson & Johnson Canada.

Natalie has been creating and teaching online Project Management courses at the undergraduate and graduate level since 2001. Needless to say, Natalie has seen her fair share of project failures and has researched many IT projects online to provide better insight on Lessons Learned in one collective piece for her graduate students as well as for you in this book.

Natalie resides in the Chesterfield Virginia area. You can connect with Natalie on LinkedIn:

https://www.linkedin.com/pub/natalie-disque-pmp/5/202/717

www.ingramcontent.com/pod-product-compliance
Lightning Source LLC
Chambersburg PA
CBHW070847180526
45168CB00002B/983